This is Daniel Cook
on a Plane

Kids Can Press

This is Daniel Cook.
He likes to go different places,
meet interesting people and
try new things.

Mostly I like to have fun!

Today Daniel is going flying.

Here we are!

This is Marty. He's a pilot.
He's going to show Daniel
some flying basics.

There are many types of planes. Passenger planes carry people. Cargo planes are like transport trucks. They move things from one place to another. Seaplanes take off and land on the water. And fighter jets are used in the military. Today Daniel is going to fly in a Cessna, a single-engine aircraft.

Super-jumbo jets can carry up to 800 people!

A Cessna is a small passenger plane. This type of Cessna is called a high-wing airplane because the wings are attached at the top of the plane.

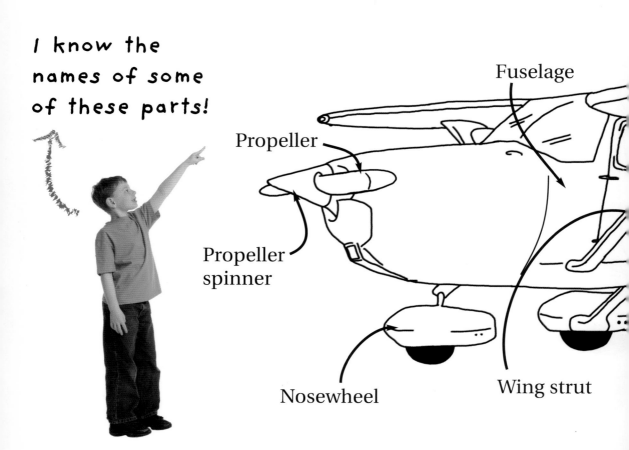

I know the names of some of these parts!

Fuselage

Propeller

Propeller spinner

Nosewheel

Wing strut

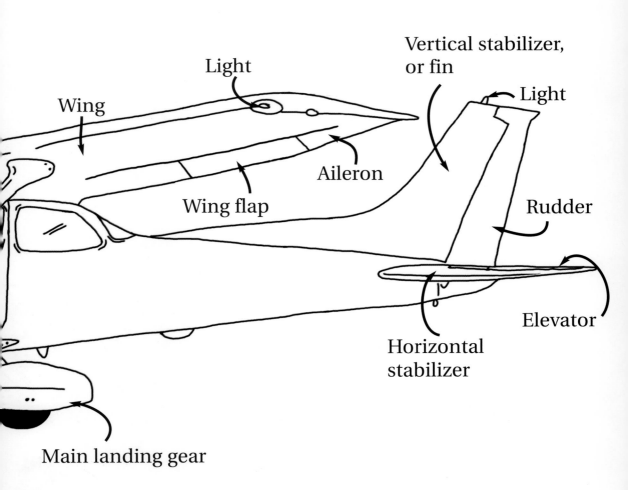

Wing

Light

Vertical stabilizer, or fin

Light

Aileron

Wing flap

Rudder

Horizontal stabilizer

Elevator

Main landing gear

Before they take off into the big blue sky, Marty and Daniel do a flight check to make sure the airplane is safe to fly.

We check for dents in the body of the plane and cracks in the windshield.

And I make sure the propeller won't get stuck.

In the cockpit,
we test the radio,
lights and wing flaps.

Check!

The doors are locked. The windows are up. Daniel has his seatbelt fastened and headset on — he's ready for takeoff!

Prop clear!

Next Marty radios the control tower for permission to move down the runway.

We got the all clear!

Marty pulls back on the control column to bring the nose of the plane up.

The control column controls the direction of the plane.

I get it — the control column is like the steering wheel in a car.

But a plane's control column can do more than turn left and right. If the pilot pulls back on it, the plane will climb. If the pilot pushes forward on it, the plane will drop.

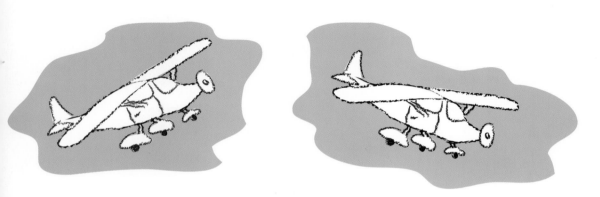

Turning the control column makes the plane roll, turning it left or right.

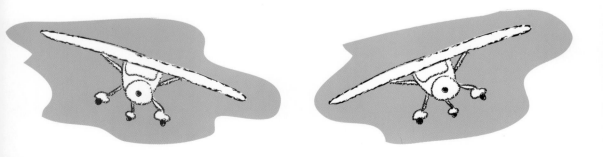

Instead of gas and brake pedals, a plane has a throttle. The pilot pushes it in to speed up during takeoff or to climb during flight. The pilot pulls it out to dive or slow down for landing.

Faster! Higher!

The instrument panel has gauges like a car's dashboard. There are six main gauges. By watching them, Marty can tell how fast he's going, how high he's flying and which direction he's heading.

The very first airplane didn't have an instrument panel — or even a cockpit! Just over a hundred years ago, Orville Wright became the first person to fly. People before him stayed up in the air with giant balloons and wind-powered gliders, but no one had figured out controlled, powered flight.

By experimenting with gliders and kites, the Wright brothers discovered that the secret was in a movable tail, movable wings and an engine.

After a few tries, Orville and Wilbur's self-built *Flyer* took off on December 17, 1903. Orville's flight lasted just 12 seconds, but it was enough to get the brothers in the history books.

Way to go, guys!

Orville's first flight proved that powered aircraft don't need wind to fly. But pilots still pay attention to the red-and-white windsock near the runway. It tells pilots which direction the wind is blowing.

Flying conditions have been great for Marty and Daniel today.

Wow! Look how high we are.

We're circling
over downtown.

It looks like
a city of ants!

Now Marty and his trusty co-pilot, Daniel, are ready to come in for a landing.

We push our control columns forward to bring the plane down — here goes!

Marty pulls the throttle out to slow the engine.

The runway's coming up fast!

Touchdown!
That was
so cool!

I learned how to fly a plane, and now it's your turn! Ready to take this super-duper paper airplane for a spin?

You will need
- a sheet of paper 22 cm x 28 cm (8 $\frac{1}{2}$ in. x 11 in.)
- clear tape, safety scissors, a ruler

1. Fold the paper in half lengthwise, then open it.

2. Can you see the fold mark from step 1? Fold the top corners into it.

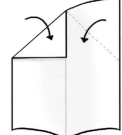

3. Now fold the top edges into the fold mark.

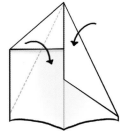

4. Fold the paper along the fold mark like you did in step 1.

5. Fold down one wing at a time so they both line up with the fold mark.

6. Bring the wings up and tape them together.

7. Make two small cuts on each side of the plane's tail. These flaps are like the Cessna's elevators — to make your plane climb, bend the flaps up.

8. If you want your plane to turn, make one small cut near the top of your plane's vertical stabilizer, or fin. This is your plane's rudder. For right turns, bend the rudder to the right. For left turns, bend the rudder to the left.

Safe flight!

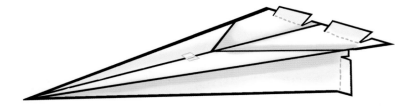

Based on the TV series *This is Daniel Cook*. Concept created by J.J. Johnson and Blair Powers. Produced by marblemedia and Sinking Ship Productions Inc.

Kids Can Press acknowledges the financial support of the Government of Ontario, through the Ontario Media Development Corporation's Ontario Book Initiative; the Ontario Arts Council; the Canada Council for the Arts; and the Government of Canada, through the BPIDP, for our publishing activity.

The producers of *This is Daniel Cook* acknowledge the support of Treehouse TV, TVOntario, other broadcast and funding partners and the talented, hard-working crew that made *This is Daniel Cook* a reality. In addition, they acknowledge the support and efforts of Deb, Murray and the Cook family, as well as Karen Boersma, Sheila Barry and Valerie Hussey at Kids Can Press.

Published in Canada by
Kids Can Press Ltd.
29 Birch Avenue
Toronto, ON M4V 1E2

Published in the U.S. by
Kids Can Press Ltd.
2250 Military Road
Tonawanda, NY 14150

www.kidscanpress.com

Written by Yvette Ghione
Edited by Karen Li
Illustrations and design by Céleste Gagnon
With special thanks to Marty Slezak and Kosta Skarlatakis of Island Flight School & Charters Inc.

Printed and bound in China

The hardcover edition of this book is smyth sewn casebound.
The paperback edition of this book is limp sewn with a drawn-on cover.

Kids Can Press is a ***lorus*™** Entertainment company

CM 06 0 9 8 7 6 5 4 3 2 1
CM PA 06 0 9 8 7 6 5 4 3 2 1

Visit Daniel online at **www.thisisdanielcook.com**

Library and Archives Canada Cataloguing in Publication
Ghione, Yvette
        This is Daniel Cook on a plane / written by Yvette Ghio

ISBN-13: 978-1-55453-081-6 (bound)
ISBN-10: 1-55453-081-4 (bound)
ISBN-13: 978-1-55453-082-3 (pbk.)
ISBN-10: 1-55453-082-2 (pbk.)

1. Airplanes—Juvenile literature.   2. Aeronautics—Juvenile literature.   3. Flight—Juvenile literature.   I. Title.

TL547.G49 2006   j629.13   C2006-900738-